GAS LIGHT & COKE

GAS LIGHT & COKE

Fergus Allen

First published in 2006 by
The Dedalus Press
13 Moyclare Road
Baldoyle
Dublin 13
Ireland

www.dedaluspress.com

ISBN 1 904556 48 5

Dedalus Press titles are represented and distributed in the USA and Canada by Dufour Editions Ltd., PO Box 7, Chester Springs, Pennsylvania 19425, and in the UK by Central Books, 99 Wallis Road, London E9 5LN

Front cover image © iStockphoto.com
Author photograph © Fergus Allen
Design by Pat Boran

Printed and bound in the UK by Lightning Source, 6 Precedent Drive, Rooksley, Milton Keynes MK13 8PR.

The Dedalus Press receives financial assistance from
An Chomhairle Ealaíon / The Arts Council, Ireland.

for Joseph Doherty

ACKNOWLEDGEMENTS

My thanks are due to the editors of the following publications in one or other of which most of these poems, or earlier versions of them, first appeared: *Times Literary Supplement; Agenda; London Magazine; Metre; Poetry Ireland Review; Poetry Review; Stand; Thumbscrew; The Waterlog* (Two Rivers Press, 2001); *'Poetry in the Parks'* (Sigma Leisure, 2000).

My warm thanks to Dennis O'Driscoll for advice.

Contents

I

II

I

Pontecorvo

Just before the car crossed Crow Bridge
haphazardness jumped out in front of us
and stopped there, dazzled by our headlights,
eyes glowing green as it raised its head.
It stood in spasm, sifting its memory
for items filed under the wrong heads,
but finding only broken wineglasses,
filaments spun by money spiders,
kindling thrown together for a bonfire,
nothing that represented order.

I said what are we going to do,
but the men in the back said drive on,
Henry James was right, you cannot help,
that is the way things are, the unwinding
goes on whether you like it or not.
So it was handbrake off, clutch out
and we accelerated up the hill,
swerving, because of wine consumed,
between one white-washed wall and another
until we reached the Palace of Culture,

lit up like an ocean liner at night,
where everything existed in categories
and was exhibited in vitrines
with labels written in Indian ink
probably back in the nineteen-twenties.
There we collected our wits and put
the episode at the bridge behind us.
The warders were charming as always,
the women sat with their knees together
and the men had seen it all before.

But while inspecting the marshalled *objets*
our thoughts drifted back to Pontecorvo,
from which even now the sound of singing
was carried up to us on the wind
with, yes, the tinkle of breaking glass.
The universe went on running down
and the citizens went on cheering
and generating their simulacra,
knowing there was still some way to go
before the approach of absolute zero.

The Fire-Escape

When it was my turn for the extension ladder
    I paused at the fifth rung from the top
To make out who was crying behind the smoke
    That rolled from a third-floor bedroom window—
A maidservant's room crammed in under the eaves
    With a view over dustbins and stables.

My gas-mask gave me the look of an intruder
    From some small but potent planet, hampered
By unfamiliar gravity and a press
    Of data, foreign and unexpected,
Weighing me down with sensations of ham-handedness
    I hadn't been briefed on in the spacecraft.

But I would recover the girl who was screaming,
    Bare-breasted and tousled at the casement.
Come, I would call out, let me salvage your body;
    When you have been washed down and sedated
I shall study your earth-perfect physiology,
    Aided by remote-handling devices.

Forty feet below devils were looking up,
    Their pale faces hung from upturned pupils.
Hoses lay around them like a disembowelment
    And the helmeted officers waited
To see you soar through a rent in reddened clouds
    With eyes raised and acquiescent hands.

The ground crew helped me to edge a little nearer
    And I could observe your desperation,
The theatrical gestures you made in earnest
    As you waited for your hidden God.
Fearing for the future of your limbs I shouted
    'Come now, child, reach out and let me take you'.

Zennor

The carved pew-end shows Morveren the mermaid
holding up a large comb and looking glass,
and, oddly enough, exposing her navel
just above the first zone of fishy scales,
which fits like a skirt for a hula-hula,
tapering off below into her tail's
curvaceousness and flare. She's bold as brass.

From evensong in St Senara's, music
spread out like mist over the rocky shore,
above all the voice of Matthew Trewella,
star of the choir and handsome as they're made.
Morveren was tickled pink by his singing,
eased herself from the chilly water, prayed
and slithered awkwardly to the west door.

She saw him. He saw her. They were fixated
and lost the use of reason as he bent
to carry her back to her natural medium,
a string of sea jade and freshwater pearls
slung artlessly around her glistening neck
and childish nape with its dark wispy curls.
She drew him gently down, and down he went,

not to be seen again, although for years
the locals heard love-cries across the bay.
Senara oversaw them and was lenient,
having herself been sentenced to be burned
for what her stepmother had called unchastity.
To save the unborn, laws were overturned,
but loose women were whores; they'd made her pay

by nailing her up inside a barrel
and casting it on to the western sea.
Inside this heaving pot she was delivered
and with the help of angels, just survived
and washed up nearly dead, the two of them,
on the far coast of Ireland, to be shrived
by an ecstatic hermit in Tralee.

I had this from the melancholy vicar,
not long back from ministering in Chad,
who stood clutching his elbows, feeling foreign,
while he spoke of Morveren and her charms—
and about indifference, a cold parish.
The only warmth was in The Tinner's Arms,
where it was alcohol that made men mad.

After Pneumonia

Convalescing in a guest house in Woodenbridge
I would sun myself on a painted seat
Under a monkey-puzzle tree and view
The Gold Mines River where it joins the Aughrim.

When lent a fishing rod I tried a cast
For some probably non-existent trout,
But at my first attempt the feathered hook
Caught among stones on the opposite bank

And could not be dislodged. My fishing days
Ended thus in a number less than one.
Or I'd dip myself into the stream's weak tea
Where it was ponded up behind some boulders

And share the stony bed with water scorpions
(Slow and harmless) and little black-green leeches
To which my lassitude would not object.
Getting out was made difficult by brambles.

When it was wet I'd play Bing Crosby records—
Lady of Spain, I Never Had a Chance—
Again and again on the wind-up gramophone
Until Mrs Byrne was fit to be tied.

The best part was the fruit garden, the gooseberries,
Hairy—not something you'd want to kiss—
But honey-yellow or a colour like vin rosé,
Waiting to have their pulp sucked out of them.

Death Sentences

Nothing original shall be written,
Let alone said or hinted at on the telephone,
Nothing that might light a lamp in the mind
Or bring back the smell of burning tobacco
Or bay rum or tomatoes in a greenhouse.
Those who condole shall do so by formula
And the replies too shall be formulaic.
Phrases drawn from the approved vocabulary
Shall be laid out quietly on his name
Like stones on a mountain cairn. In public
The survivors must not be moved to tears.
Then it's back to the house and sleeping tablets
And later the stimulants as prescribed.

In other countries, of course, they beat their breasts
And scream and fling themselves down on the coffin,
And no one thinks it odd or is embarrassed.
Just the reverse, bewailing a lost love
(That is to say, a person who was loved)
Is the most natural thing in the afterworld.

But try not to follow him down to Hades,
He will already have turned the corner
And, yes, when you get there in your turn
The path will be empty, though the air's movement
May tell you he recently passed that way.

Therimenes

After this agreement Therimenes handed over the fleet to Astyochus.
He sailed away himself in a small boat and was lost at sea.

— Thucydides, VIII, 38

They reached Miletus shortly after noon,
All eighty ships, in no sort of formation,
Now safely tethered in the anchorage,
Their manifests and bills of lading ready
For the Spartan admiral's approbation.

The status quo was just what he'd expected,
All to cock as ever, everyone fighting
Everyone else, Athenians in Samos,
Tissaphernes waving a bag of bribes
And an earthquake to make it more exciting.

They'd shown no interest in his adventures,
What he'd achieved, his views about the war
Or how the victualling had gone in Leros.
No one had thanked him, offered him a drink
Or even recommended him a whore.

Next morning, then, he walked down to the harbour.
Nobody was about. His former crews
Had spent the night whooping it up with men
Who served Astyochus and now lay sleeping
In the Milesian alleyways and stews.

So that was it. Two great fleets brought together
Out of the Peloponnese and Syracuse,
Shepherded across the bloody Aegean—
And he could now push off to where he came from.
What he had done would never count as news.

Astyochus had made his deal with Darius,
Now it was clearly time to cut and run.
The mastic trees were oozing in the fields
Like agéd men with sores, the lop-eared goats
Stared insolently at him in the sun.

A small caique to take him to Laconia
Was all he could afford, a crew of two
And rations that would help them to survive
As far as Naxos with a bit of luck;
From there the gods would tell them what to do.

The locals on the quay watched him cast off
And waved him a perfunctory farewell
While they were grilling squid and pouring wine.
Eyes on the west, on the qui vive to spy
Not Aphrodite floating on a shell

But the faint outline of a childhood cliff
With stone pines in a row along the top,
Therimenes steered for the sunset, gruff
To his shipmates, resentment in his heart.
Home was to be the first and only stop.

Two days out, with slate clouds overhead, lightning
Let fly, Zeus shook a thunder-sheet offstage,
Wind struck them like a pillow and they reeled;
The boat turned turtle, left them thrown and floundering;
Poseidon played, Aeolus turned the page.

Like sailors everywhere they couldn't swim,
The crewmen roared and sank; defiant still
Therimenes clung weakening to a spar,
Then thought of now, opened a crying mouth
And swallowed the future against his will.

11

Syracuse

Sitting in the Greek theatre in Neapolis
with the sun dazzling my eyes, unaware
of shades of the Hellenic dead—yes, there
at last is the great harbour, right ahead of me.
This is the moment to think about Nicias

and his Athenian fleet, soon to be vanquished,
the remnants still lying on the bed after,
what, nearly two and a half thousand years,
amphorae intact, unused spearheads greened,
even some human bones among the strakes.

I myself see only a dead arena
flat on its back with open arms, a motor boat
tethered amid the glitter of the wavelets,
an aircraft overhead. The rest is literature
and traces in my brain. Food would be welcome.

In Ortygia after wine and fish
the view is rosier, the Duomo beckons
from the rhetorical baroque façade
of Andrea Palma, with its gowned saints,
broken pediments, the theatre of Christ—

just scenery. Behind it stands old truth
among the Doric columns that enshrined
Athene and her strategy in war.
Here Dionysius the tyrant venerated
the hidden goddess dwelling like a pupa,

self-absorbed, in this mysterious naos.
Though seated in what was a sacred space,
suitable emotions do not arise in me,
the ancient transmitters are off the air,
there's truly stony silence and indifference.

I've known places of execution, circuses,
similarly silent, always preoccupied
with their continuing pasts. So today
The fleet continues to sink in the harbour,
The sailors are still dying in the quarry.

Irises

The brown-eyed women wave expressive hands
In front of their huge curvilinear busts,
Reliving feelings felt in crises past.

It's Minerva, the Blue-eyed Maid, who sees
An ice-floe floating south, a polar bear
Hollow-sided and carried towards Cancer.

On the Island

I

The track down to the estuary zig-zagged
Between spurs and outcrops of old red sandstone.
Some kind of St John's Wort lived on the verges
Along with thistles, which the bees preferred.

At low tide the bladderwracks lay flat out
Like a colony of sunbathing seals
On the ever wet rocks, but come high water
They were showing off their nymphean hair,

Which caught in our blades as we rowed across,
Half-seas-over, to the camp on the island.
The landing-place was buttery with mud—
Roux spilt twice daily on a kitchen floor—

Which led to many unamusing incidents
On the irregular steps. From the ridge
One could, when sober, make out other islands
With Anglicized names and five-star hotels,

Whose patrons, while not positively wicked,
Enjoyed having a large slice of the cake.
But their bracken, like ours, was full of ticks,
Which burrowed into the midriff and itched.

That, at three in the morning, was a comfort.
Not long after dawn a fishing boat, drab,
With a matchboarded wheel-house up forrad,
Would wake me with the throbbing of its motor,

Rounding the point and setting sail for Crete,
Fate, not to be spoken to, at the helm.
In fact they were going for flatfish, followed
Of course by the usual gang of gulls

And getting back after the flood set in.
Sometimes I'd wave, and once I thought a pipe
Was raised in acknowledgement, though the face
Stayed hidden behind the salt-frosted glass.

The jetty where they moored was out of sight
And the crew never showed up at Winnie's pub,
So the mystery of real life going on
While we wasted our portion remained unsolved.

There were days when the crowd from the Majestic
Would descend from Olympus and go whizzing past
With outboard motors, faces turned away—
No doubt thinking we looked rather unsavoury.

Their cries from downstream, mostly corybantic,
Suggested a party among the rushes,
With high voices—reminders of the parrot house—
Wafting across the monkey island moat.

Our companions the voles paid no attention,
Squatting near the water to wash their faces,
But I sat and smoked among the gorse bushes
In my usual state of discontent.

II

Having each other, the pair who were with me
Seemed not to know whose eyes the sun was shining from;
I was on my own, with notebook and hangover,
Watching the future emerge from the rain.

Once a dredger tied up across the water,
Its grab rattled up and own for a week
Dragging out the earth's entrails, to deposit them
Abruptly in the barge tethered alongside.

And not a man to be seen, just machinery
Marking the hours with its torturer's gestures,
And everything looking the same, no spasms
As the roads to salvation were reshaped.

But down below, the bloody-minded currents
Soon went back to their childhood ways
And were crossing themselves and genuflecting
And invoking the holy name in crises.

Before that, though, the deepened shipping channel
Made life easier for the coastal traffic,
The little tanker with heating oil and petrol
That chugged past us every other Tuesday

And the freighter from Par with kaolin
For a pottery where the clay is forced
To adopt configuratons of piety.
Their bows cleft the silty water like crocodiles

Homing in on a wounded buffalo
That struggled despairingly miles upstream—
Not evil, simply enacters of programmes
That make the phenomenal world exciting.

III

This island is not much more than a rock.
I can scramble from one end to the other
In the time my friends take to love and honour
Their reflections shivering in a puddle.

Now and again a turnstone may show up
To forage among the barnacled boulders,
Where later the incoming tide will run
As the reaches fill up with foreign salt,

But the thought of a diet of periwinkles
Is enough to send me back to the mainland
And survival among vocation-seekers
When the leaves are falling in Stephen's Green.

All along, over the cambered horizon,
Marine monsters are travelling across
The sea's surface on their sinuous bellies,
Exhaling puffs of superheated steam,

And in the four corners the heads of small
Decapitated boys are blowing gales
Suited to the canvas of any navigator.
They are carrying Theseus on his way

To put an end to the poor deformed creature
Pent up inside Minos's stinking labyrinth,
Dreaded and loathed, what should have been aborted.
That done the boys and girls can set off home

And after Naxos sing without inhibition.
The fishing boat seems to carry a sail,
But the sea glitters and against the light
I can't be sure whether it's black or white.

Blue Sky

This morning's blue sky is decorated
with a flotilla of light-headed clouds.

Mass-produced and uniformly spaced,
they diminish towards the horizon
according to the rules of perspective
and define a sexless elevation
where our obsessions no longer matter.

The airworthy birds are in between,
neither with us nor of us, but waiting
to reassert themselves in the pecking order
when our roughshod riding has provoked
uprising from all sides and below.

Into this space aeroplanes descend
and let themselves drone lumpishly down
on to concrete stained by fear and hope.

Homunculi emerge from the hatches,
calculating their financial futures.

And up above, up there, the ice particles
do their best to rearrange themselves
so that no resemblance can be seen
to the shapes of camels, whales or weazels.

Either way the gent behind the arras
will be stuck by the thinking man's épée.

At the Meeting of the Niles

Where the not very coloured waters mix
  And a brown young man in a cotton nightshirt
Is poling his something like a canoe
  Along the more or less decayed revetment

The White Nile merges itself with the Blue.
  My upbringing tells me to disregard
The clamour at the far end of the street
  That sounds like 'Down, down with the USA'.

Sang froid comes from the lands of snow and sleet
  And my passport is meant to be my breastplate,
But I doubt if this is a reading rabble—
  To them my papers will be double Dutch

And my face the image of Western babble
  About freedom and the capital market.
And tonight, when the moon races through rack
  And my French window trembles in the khamsin,

Will they come raging and hating in black
  Balaclavas, wordlessly smashing in?
No, no, that would have to be nearer home—
  Christendom and the provinces of faith

Anywhere from the Bible belt to Rome.
  Here violence is always done in white
In the name of Him whom there's no one but.
  The palm-trees are clattering in the wind

And the hotel's gopher-wood doors are shut;
  The air is dry and silent in the corridor
And the servant not to be seen, asleep
  Perhaps, or on the streets, flourishing keys.

The expatriates' paleface children weep
  With apprehension in their lonely beds
As the open throats draw gradually near,
  Hollering their way down the dusty boulevard

And then recede, leaving fuses of fear
  To smoulder in the compounds of the rich.
Sleep like a sea-mist blows across my mind,
  Then suddenly it's day and the first aircraft

Are slithering down through the dusty wind
  To subside bumpily on to the runway.
So despite the dark looks and detonations,
  The smoke hesitating over the Residence

And the recurrent blood-chilling ovations,
  There may be someone who uses my tongue
And will transport me to another latitude,
  Where my body, naked and pale, may vegetate

And my animula assume an attitude
  Of piety, though not in the Land of Punt
Or even in the Land of Steady Habits,
  Where live poets might peer over my shoulder.

Gas Light & Coke

It was after we'd crossed the Royal Canal
that we got the feel of the country's otherness,
people so chilly they were forced to burn
the land they lived on, chopped up into sods,
which they had to dry in the dark wet summers.
One day they would have consumed their smallholdings.

We by contrast were always warm and comfortable,
looked after by the Gas Light & Coke Company
(whose works on Misery Hill we avoided,
not liking the dust and the smell of sulphur).
As we walked our setter along the front,
discussing the heavy going at Leopardstown,

newsmens' flashes flickered across the sky,
as though triggered by angels on the prowl
for evidence to aid the prosecution.
A bolt stabbed the West Pier's finger tip, dousing
the light, while boulders rolled above our heads
and downpours soaked us, clad in tweed and voile.

Once home, the Gas Light & Coke Co took charge,
heated the baths, warmed up the Turkish towels
and made ice for our preprandial drinks.
Not that we took it for granted. Pathetic
turf-cutters were ever in our thoughts, as
were the confessors who kept them in order.

And the Pigeon House raised a smoky finger,
as though advising us against disdain.
Meantime Bray Head with a chip on its shoulder
frowned its Pre-Cambrian frown, while it tolerated
the chairoplanes and the side-show of freaks.
Where in the compass would salvation come from?

Round the horizon, north, south, east and west,
the band of sky was theatrically bright
with the cheerfulness of departing guests,
while overhead the clouds were like a lid
Under which we citizens, rich or shabby,
waited with disquiet, as in a stockyard.

How the Mind Works

Sometimes I would say a word to myself
over and over and over, or read it repeatedly,
hearing it in my mind, until the sense
had been sublimed like a crystal of iodine
from a crucible over a Bunsen burner.

In the classroom, staring through Waterford rain
across the hockey pitch, the inner voice
to which I listened might murmur dogma, dogma,
dogma, dogma—or therapy, therapy, therapy—
until every whisper of meaning had been lost.

So you might say the word's silken cocoon
had been unravelled, the hull stripped off,
revealing sticks of syllables
and a pale, motionless pupa, its eyes closed,
wings never yet unfolded.

Later, with pictures, it was much the same.
Life with Boldini's *Lady Colin Campbell*
changed from a vision of class and *volupté*
to little but interwoven brushstrokes
of black and flesh caught on the tooth of canvas,

the tempting imago all but invisible.
And then there was the girl in whose overstudied face
I could in the end see only consuming pupils—
and made my escape by saying over
words like devotion and conjugality.

Cheap Music

The dance music I heard at seventeen—
Seventy-eights cleverly rerecorded
So that the soliciting tunes and harmonies
Circulate in my antiquated cochlea
More or less as they did in the year dot
And speak of the real girls of then, not
Shadows and highlights moving on a screen:

I knowingly give myself up to this,
To a style I was taught to disappprove of,
A style I first tried on like lipstick in puberty
And loved the taste and feel of, being hidden
Behind a mask designed for years ahead—
The slice of life enacted in the bed,
The thing beyond come-hither and a kiss.

And the voices—snapshots of vapour trails,
Whose sources were left behind in mid-century,
Where, mopping and mowing among themselves
In crêpe-de-Chine and artificial silk,
They cluster beneath art deco chandeliers
And reminisce about their voguish years
Before fashion left them with flapping sails.

Nostalgia of this kind resembles gin,
More of a depressant than an elixir.
Better stick to the tea of Nuwara Eliya
Or coffee mouldy from the wharves of Malabar—
That way the bodies lying in the street
Will not be overlooked or naked feet
Lack sympathy to warm their frostbite in.

MD

All over the known world tarry sailors
Are making landfalls and dropping anchor
To put ashore golden-eyed adventurers,
Complete with crucifixes and kindling.

How far they'll get with their leaky boots,
Fantasy maps and rations of biscuit
Seems to depend as much on mosquitoes
As on the hours devoted to prayer

(Of which there are fewer than reported).
Anyway our ships bring home the bullion,
Some of it in diabolic shapes,
Though the smelter rapidly returns it

To the forms ordained by mindless nature.
(We, contemporaries of Erasmus,
Aren't so fussy about this today,
As a banker's view of gold evolves.)

Generally things are looking good:
The half-millenium has arrived
And not too many people are making
Donkeys and pig's arses of themselves

As they did back in AD one thousand.
Natural philosophy is explaining
Things and events that used to seem magical,
Reason graciously ascends the throne

And now we've simply got to fill in
The blanks in our knowledge of the world—
Which is routine work for clever hacks.
The ideal state is within our grasp

And bliss awaits future generations.
Why there are nights when we dream of happenings
Before they come to pass is a mystery,
But the alchymists will answer that one.

We get all our necessary pepper
Somewhere beyond the Straits of Malacca
And the best of our steel from Toledo;
With these we can prick both tongues and hearts.

Looking back through figurative telescopes
On centuries blighted by untestable
Theory and a fear of observation,
We give thanks at being spared the darkness.

True enough, we have our growing pains,
But we've reached a plateau, over which
We can march with pale and smiling faces
Towards what will soon be called Utopia.

Bougainvillea

for Paul Roche

Philibert Commerson, the botanist, found it
In Brazil and knew it was something special,
With its overwhelming magenta bracts
And tiny flowers, easily overlooked
By retinas punch-drunk with so much colour—
Miniature daisy-faced things, like the eyes
Of mock-innocent actresses and vamps,
For whom the dazzle equalled a disguise.

Bougainville was intrigued—the Royal Society
Must be informed, when they got back to France;
Meanwhile their frigate, *La Boudeuse,* well stocked
With light hearts, salted mutton and clean water,
Must hasten southwards to Magellan's Straits,
The longed-for Pacific and the savage isles
That he would claim in the name of Louis Quinze—
Often *en passant,* saving lives and miles.

Months later in Port Louis du Bouchage
Poor seasick Commerson took himself off,
But before leaving said: mon capitaine,
Cher maitre (or suchlike), I propose to name,
With your permission, this enchanting vine
After the Bougainvilles, of whom the flower
Must be your mathematical brute self,
With your enlightenment, ambition, power.

Easterly

A cold April, and worse coming if I
interpreted the Mongolian forecast
correctly. However, the Inxian mountains
are not where I'm heading, or so I hope.

The black sheep have paused by the willow wood
and are looking at me over their mud-flecked
haunches. Is he a threat, they ask themselves,
and, being cautious ovines, answer yes.

But from among the trees a man in denim
appears and hollers at me with nasal vowels.
Incomprehensible. I smile and gesture
in the soothing way that foreigners have.

He repeats himself, then touches my elbow,
signing to follow him to his earth house.
So who lies here, stretched on a cot, her pupils
fluttering like a bird trapped behind lids

resolved to hold the soul within the body?
It is the orphan niece, always the niece,
descended out of a variant line,
whose genes give rise to offspring that attract

the unstable nucleus in the male.
And I am not immune. St Patrick's breastplate
will hardly shield me from the lethal doses
being emitted by her seed of radium.

A youth wearing a weedy black moustache
enters, wrapped up in irrational anger
or some kind of home-made jealousy, shouting
at the country odalisque and her minder.

I back out slowly through the summer fly screen,
turn and run to the charcoal-burner's clearing
to recover my round-rumped little horse.
Bareback we trot, no, canter to the lamasery,

where I resume my spiritual exercises,
soon rising up like a hot air balloon
into a zone silent as outer space,
but for the fitful roar of my own burners.

The Unadapted

I fly in the troughs of the waves
but the manx shearwater passes me by.

I hide myself among bars of shadow
but the tiger easily makes me out,

the insects register my movements
and the blindworm knows regardless.

Legs straight I can barely touch my toes
but the garter snake gets itself knotted.

Seeing me swimming in the harbour
the fish would laugh if they were able.

While I am fumbling for my key
the cockroach slithers under the door

and the mouse vanishes into the skirting,
her movements quick as mercury.

I am cold. I want to wear your fleece
and requisition your windbreak.

These raw roots and limpets make me sick,
but my fire has died among its ashes

and Lord lightning has not struck again.
In any case the undergrowth is soaking.

Cheerless, yes. But that's not the end of me—
something you will all be sorry to hear.

Grandfathers

Dragged offstage before my birth,
The bodies had been disposed of,
A modus vivendi reached,
A pact initialled sight unseen.
Little was said in my presence;
When alluded to, the dead
Were named in a loving tone,
But many unuttered thoughts
Floated like overfed putti
Around the coves of the ceiling,
Speaking to me by telepathy.

The bottle had dragged them down
After years of rage and misery.
Passing the propped-open doors
Of Whelan's pub and the sickening
Smell of last night's beer and whiskey,
I see the off-duty curate
With his grease-grey mop asperging
The floorboards, messed by togetherness,
Mucus and other unspeakables.
The smell would be of carbolic
And insufferable sanctity.

The wine merchant, too, had sent
His Christmas-box case of claret—
Bottles of blood for the sufferer
When his head-bands grew unbearable.
The other side of the fire
Disapproval sat in black
With common sense on her side
And a drought between her legs,
While the men of God declined
To give evidence for life,
Invoking the fifth amendment.

So where did the pink house go to—
Pink-washed roughcast with a fanlight—
And the sober-looking pony,
The whippet and the canary
And the apple tree that featured
In all the family photographs?
Down the shore in the floodwater's
Spate, carrying away feculence,
Matchsticks and the head of Orpheus
That cried out so inconsolably
At the family's dismemberment.

And much the same for the Cornishman,
Who exiled himself from Camborne
And foundered off the ice-shelf
Of South London in the gales
That blew behind frosted glass.
But their childrens' childish memories
Were of affectionate fathers.
The terrible nights came later,
Statues reeling off their plinths,
The mantles of the gaslights
Broken and collecting dust.

The relicts had to limp onwards
With their unknowing offspring
Through gardens of convalescence—
One child, me, without old men
To tell him that nothing mattered.
Aged orphan, I wonder who
Were these not so wise old owls
Addicted to self-destruction,
Men who gave me half my genes,
My eyebrows, perhaps my fingernails,
My neural pathways, my thinking.

Amateur snaps show geniality
And bushy moustaches, heads
Tilted slightly to the left,
Tolerant of unsure eyes
Hovering above the viewfinder
And forefingers feeling blindly
For the nib that clicked the shutter.
But nothing more. Sepia images
Of postures and clothes and hints
Of flesh and hair, from which soul
Has vaporized like alcohol.

They're still there, part of me thinks,
Detained under house arrest
In their own segment of space-time,
Cloistered, incommunicado,
But unquiet in their quarantine
And quite without curiosity
About the never heard of me.
Anyway what would we talk about?
Our mutually strange diction
And bearing would come between us,
With translators' comic errors.

My one grandson has one grandfather,
Who survives up on the terraces,
On the lookout for a lodging.
And despite what count as quirks
In the eyes of friends and villagers,
I can still walk a chalk line
When challenged by the police,
Speechifying while I do so
About the ruses of time
And the interpenetration
Of the now by what was then.

Battue

The origami-master folded away his smile
And swept his extended family into the litter-bin
To be eaten by paper tigers.

A Bad Debt (1842)

i.m. Robert Allen

Robert under the greening larches,
he aging, yes, he poorly, yes.
And a stream, hobbled by hazels,
boisterous down the slade,
under the mill and into the Nore—
nearly if not quite 'sylvan beauty'.
And friend Frederick, old corn-factor,
he beg Robert to stand security
for airiest venture yet.

Robert not friendly but grumpy,
shows bare willing. Signs he note of hand
and goeth back to his mill.
Frederick fails, has always failed,
has the judgement of an old boot.
Comes then the Bank of New Ross.

Robert, he without reserves,
he no pay. Is dunned, despairs
to be shamed before Inistioge.
Barbiturates not yet invented, acushla
(where did you pick up that horrible word?).
Grimly grabs gun from cupboard,
recites him words from Bible,
blows out brains in study.

Over the hill comes he galloping,
brother John from New Ross,
panting with good newsworth,
debt paid, all well, all happy.
That moment gun goes slam. Oh no,
no for goodwife Mary Louisa, relict now,
no for five young daughters in a row.

Now modern charley, fixed focus man,
he and wife see ghost, last Wednesday week
and all holidays of obligation.
Not Robert, no, sleeps he well,
but grey lady, lady in grey (corny),
in long long dress, you know,
moving across study, door to wall
(but say nothing in front of the child).

Exmoor

Exmoor Hunt pipe tobacco was the incongruous
Smoke favoured by my older friend, who sat
Surrounded by pictures collected in Prague,
Allowing himself an after-dinner puff
While Enid played Liszt on the Bosendorfer.
Exmoor would not have been Leslie's cup of tea.
(When his wife tried to seduce me, I resisted,
Not caring much for women in trousers.)

But Coleridge's company he might have liked.
Having translated Hegel, he inclined
To speculation, and STC in spate
On the transcendental features of the sundew
(A plant I've seen kerb-crawling not far from Simonsbath)
Would have turned his mind to *Naturphilosophie*.
And a touch of sunburn had its appeal,
Connected in some way with youths in Sparta.

Without the two of them the world is barer,
The wind sighs over the moorland reservoirs
Where sightless willows are delicately feeling
The faces of the water, wistful for features
That will tell them what all of us want to hear.
Way off to the west, beyond Lundy, stratified
Clouds with curling edges bar the sun—
And here comes the Exmoor Hunt (but not much cheering).

Grinzing

I think, uh, I think it's—if I knew how to start—
But it has, had, well yes has, it's eating me up,
To do with your, our, the space between us these days,
It's not easy to say this, uh, say it with people
In the corner looking over (please nod and smile
If you follow me) what I mean is in some ways

Things, you could uh, make believe they're the same as ever,
I can't find the words, the quite right words, but you know,
I'm sure you've uh, guessed what I'm—oh it's something new.
Last week when we were dancing, danced, you wore the velvet
And the steps were the old steps, not what they do now,
Black velvet, or was it damson, or navy blue,

But soft, it was the touch, feel, coming through my fingers
And our bodies remembering familiar programmes,
Yes we'll have, yes, another carafe of the red,
But it wasn't the same, not the same, not like Grinzing
And you never looked into my, no you, uh, looked
Over my shoulder, if it was something I said,

And it's true I can—oh, but that's not what it is,
Is it, it's that cousin of yours I caught a glimpse of
Beside you in the Augustinerkirche, calm
But getting ready to pounce, just when I turned up
Without warning and late for the Mozart Requiem
And Hübner's setting of the, uh, Ninetieth Psalm.

The Abalone Handlers

Amidships on some sort of inshore yawl
A man in oilskins reaches out a hand
To steady his mate as he tries to grab
The cable from a dredge, which drips and trails
Green and burgundy strands of living matter.

Before them an anxious girl of eleven
In an incongruously flowered dress
Holds out a bundle of what might be sandwiches,
And a bright-eyed dog, eager about everything,
Rears and yaps to little or no effect,

But might dart in among the yellow legs.
Dumped at their feet the dredge's jaws disgorge
An assortment of bewildered crustaceans,
Who scratch their way slowly across the deck,
Half-seas-over from gravity and air.

Splashes sound nearby on the right, a diver
Surfaces at a ladder, pannier crammed
With dripping hand-sized abalone molluscs,
Red ones and pink; lifts arm, waves a gloved fist;
The two trawlers hoick him out by the elbows.

These are hard currency; stacked in the kitchens
Of waterfront restaurants they will bait
The menus for the show-offs and their lovers.
(Fingers around a wine-glass flash with diamonds,
Daddy with a peasant's complexion pays.)

For now the diver bares his head and breathes;
The yellow legs busy themselves with crates;
The terrier eats the sandwiches; the child
With mock expressions of disgust and fear
Scoops two lobsters into a plastic bag.

An Assumption

Today I decided to become a god.
No one had asked me, but things had gone to pot,
girls were no longer seeing me in the street
(had I, I sometimes wondered, become invisible?)
and thoughts that used to appeal were now unwelcome,
as to a vegetarian the thought of meat.

Emptiness, too, was flowing into the house
faster than I could brush it out of the door.
The best escape was to rise above it all,
using self-help techniques that are kept a secret
only from people who do not wish to know.
As the flood waters went swirling through the hall

I lay against the ceiling like a balloon
and stared down upon the furniture that floated
and jostled its way into the open air,
while the weathermen barked about days to come.
Like the bright-eyed arsenic-eaters of Styria,
known for their unforced breathing and lustrous hair,

they spoke of time as though it travelled like water,
always downhill, from the higher to the lower.
But then I moved on to the unsaddling yard,
where, free of blinkers, I could peacefully sweat
and be teased and even prodded with a stick
by those who'd spotted a stumer on the card.

As for the highest level [*deleted, censor*] ...
but the food is good and everyone is kind.
Your fear that aloneness lay in store was wrong
(think of Elysium and the goings-on there);
in fact the place is chock-a-block—and the queue
for the return journey infinitely long.

42

The Iron Room

An iron room like this must have been made
Circa 1900 by workers used
To riveting the hulls of merchant ships.
The thickly painted walls are surely bulkheads
And the half-inch steel door, with its inertia
And screw-down handle the size of a dinner plate,
Is as undomesticated as anything.
But there's no good reason to feel afraid.

It looks like just the place to store your gold
And other valuables of a personal nature—
A hidey-hole of secret satisfaction.
All the same the complete absence of windows
And adequate seating lowers the spirits.
From the ventilator grille in the ceiling
Issue noises more animal than mineral,
As it might be from creatures in the hold.

Not cosy, then, but seemingly secure,
In spite of the continuous vibration,
Unsteady deck and footsteps overhead.
If there were any openings or portholes
What would you see (if you'd the words to say)?
Maybe this express delivery service
Preserves you like an artificial womb
Until the signal comes to go ashore.

The Wicket

Having received the password I'm unsure
(as always) where I'm now allowed to go:
could my, er, doppelgänger sign the register
in a love hotel (payment in advance)?
It could? Perhaps. But my personal liking
is for the shaded room, the glass half-empty,
the cat musing on the sofa, forepaws tucked
neatly under, enjoying his sinecure.

Now I speak the formula at the grille
and brace myself to suffer whatever offers,
however outlandish or highly coloured.
First comes the world as the police must see it,
the guilty and the blameless quite distinct;
then an unknown woman in moiré silk
begs me to pose inside her jeweller's shop
as a bulldog in a raincoat, dressed to kill,

or as a décoy among the top-lit cases
glittering like diamanté whelk-stalls
before the wishful eyes of passers-by.
It's my dull appearance that's so reassuring,
the respectablility, the viscous flow,
nothing could run crookedly in my slack veins.
Or that is how she sees me; and maybe rightly,
perhaps our spirits are truly in our faces.

Hold me up to a mirror: my fishlike lips
droop at the expectation of days to come,
time dribbles from the corners of my mouth.
The password has come too late, and being spoken
opens more doors than one. Out in the bog

that tussock has the look of terra firma,
but gives way under the pressure of the foot;
up to the knees I'd go, or up to the hips

or further, but for the bleep of my sixth sense.
The wicket gate opens away from me, making
retreat more difficult, maybe impossible,
if the smell of the future should turn me off.
I should never have signed up, never consented
to let my name go forward. Better to live
with oil lamps, drawing water from the well
in iron buckets, sitting on the fence.

Penguin Island

Advised to keep the outboard motor running
because of the penguins, I look again
and there indeed are penguins in their thousands,
like duckweed on a pond. From where I'm standing
on a point of the ragged basalt coastline
after a hazardous approach and landing
they have taken over these inshore waters.
Once stalled, restarting among such a throng
would bother me; I leave the motor running.

Inland the typically maritime grass
is short, flat on the ground, chromium green
and spattered with penguin droppings (white);
penguins stand around, getting through their lives,
and the air is filled with the smell of fish oil
and decaying crab. Lichen just survives.
Human habitations, built with the leg-bones
of giant flightless birds, long since extinct,
lie in ruins on the polluted grass.

A one-time whaling station? Who's to know?
Maybe a party of mutinous sailors
was marooned here with half a keg of powder
and a single musket—and left to waste,
even turn cannibal before they perished.
But these penguins' forebears were never chased,
clubbed or eaten, and their fearless offspring
now estimate me with their orange eyes,
knowing something I shall never know.

The clouds pile up, the motor coughs and fails
and, as I watch, the penguins overrun
my black inflatable and foul her cockpit.
But the distant mother-ship spreads her arms
and beckons to me with her Aldis lamp.
Her mastery and fire-power calms
my venturer's disquiet, while she sends
a pinnace to recall me and my notebook
before the miserable daylight fails.

In the Hotel

Round the corner from the passenger lift
The goods lift waited with its door wide open
While two blue-jeaned removal men attempted
To shift a bulky something in or out.
Whatever it was, it was tightly wrapped,
But metallic corners and knobs protruded,
Catching the lintel at each push or heave
Or getting themselves wedged between the jambs.
When tilted, loose parts slid about inside,
And a sickening odour filled the lobby.

Damage having been done, the men revolted
And crashed the thing slantwise into the lift,
Where it's impact quivered the chandelier
And alarmed the guests, all of whom then peered
Into the cage, to see what lay there, static,
Its doors wide open—with a human body
Visible face down among foreign rugs.
It fell to the police to turn him over
And show the shabby clothes, the black moustache,
The eyes closed down into a sallow face.

His papers were beyond us, words unreadable,
In a tongue officially known as hard.
Then we were told to leave, and plastic tape
Marked off what was called the 'incident area'.
But the face remained with us, like a haunting,
As of a being with a mask not ready
To revert to the state of lifeless matter,
Saying, hang on, I've yet to make my point—
But emblematic of a man misled
(As we all of us find ourselves misled).

Storyville Portraits

Three dozen images of prostitutes
In New Orleans, nineteen-twelve:
Some clothed, others naked as eggs,
All showing themselves to the camera
For motives we can only guess at.

Their faces, whether sportive, pert,
Demure, grasping or self-defensive,
Invite stereotyped responses;
Their dear but unoriginal bodies
Say what has oft been said before.

More provocative are the wallpapers,
The late Victorian chaises longues,
The whatnots, necklaces and oleographs
And, on one or two of the girls,
Indisputable hammer-toes.

Their parlours look tired in the daylight,
For who will trouble to maintain
Outposts convention has abandoned?
But these are theatres where the lighting
Is in the hands of the distillers;

Mint juleps are always in fashion
For the ladies, and rye or bourbon
For the gentlemanly clientèle,
Who will later spill their slurred consonants
Over the bedspreads and pillowcases.

Spare us your caring condescension,
They would probably say. OK,
But what gives me the feel of velvet
Stroked against the lie of the fabric
Are these bare bodies, with their skins

Like peeled mushrooms ready for cooking,
Seated there before the photographer
Among the respectable chattels,
The embroidered throws on the tables,
The Turkey carpets, the carved walnut.

They take me aback, as an idler
Might be taken aback while chatting,
If his wandering hand encountered
A dead goldfish, even a frog,
In that dusty old fur-lined teacup.

Anxiety

Annie's pubic hair was beyond a joke.
A few graceful alpines are always welcome,
But tropical rainforest takes getting used to.

Doing my best to advance through the dark
My bull's-eye showed up nothing but lianas
And resistant tendrils in all directions.

Could there be dangerous animals here,
I asked myself, or might I catch a fever
Or run into a lurking lepidopterist?

I hesitated to think what hidden adit
Led into that promising hillside, calling
For resolution, Davy lamp, canary.

First Thing

Like a marine worm sensitive to light
I feel day break beyond the bedroom curtains,
A region of air signalling its whereabouts
To a diver who ascends among bubbles
From a once-again unrewarded search
For missing bullion. Admiralty charts
Are true and beautiful, but bound as always
By the Official Secrets Act and therefore
Not to be trusted when it's them or us.

The sea-floor is occupied by the past.
The barely visible boat-decks and funnels
Way down below me in the scattered light,
Grey and encrusted and part of the scenery
Only for local fish, carry me back
To those parental ships I thought the world of,
Or possibly they're what's left of a temple
Dedicated to a genus of gods
That disappeared with the rest of Gondwanaland.

But day weighs in like an overdue tanker,
Its bow wave rocks the dinghies in the harbour,
Dragging foam and flotsam along the mole
As I leap forward into daytime life,
Into the fraternity of antagonisms
And the incessant reshaping of matter.
Across the road young girls in cotton dresses
Smile among themselves in the early sunshine,
But they head south and I am walking north.

The Dartry Dye Works

I ofen walked past the Dartry Dye Works,
three storeys of dark limestone, known as calp,
the name spelled out in large capital letters
of blue and white enamel—

D
A
R
T
R
Y

D
Y
E

W
O
R
K
S

It was just to the right beyond the tram sheds

where the tarred road sloped down to the Dodder
(a river liable to flashy floods
from its heathery catchment in Glencree).
Ash and sycamores stood around it, breathing;
I never saw anyone leave or enter,
but steam often flowed from a rusty pipe
that stuck out sideways through the north wall,
so there was surely something going on.

I now believe they only dyed things black.
That would be for the aftermath of death
and to see people through their times of mourning.
Once black, of course, there was no reverting
to burgundy or beige or powder blue,
which explains all those sombre-looking people
hanging around the Lower Rathmines Road
after making their vows and intercessions.

There is never any shortage of blackness
among the stage props of revealed religions.
Blackness is something abstract, like an absence;
but on nights without stars or electricity
when the curtained sky is up to nothing,
the pupils of a dreamer's eyes can shrink
against the glare of sunlight on a hillside
across which he finds himself on the move.

Reaching a station is not the end, though,
only another beginning, from which
he sets off once more in the wrong direction.
There are no seats, no bulbs in the light-sockets
and the tunnel is tortuous and black.
Emerging into unprepared-for light
the world he finds himself in is the image
of the one he left with such a commotion.

Deep under his feet in dolomite caves
explored only by hearty speleologists
lives a creature, *Leucippus*, pale and blind,
the size of his little finger with legs,
whose life is lived as though in Indian ink.
Slithering gingerly through the lime water,
black is a word for which it has no use.
Nor is absence what it would call its lot.

In the abyssal trench it's much the same;
phosphorescence is merely self-advertisement,
not a lighting up of dismal surroundings;
while the drizzle of decomposing debris
from those that feed and spawn up there in daylight
is little more than fertilizing rain
falling in endless night. So black is best—
to which I'd add least seen, soonest forgotten.

Another just invented motto says
the sweetest songs come from the blackest birds.
In Palmerston Park they whistled their titles
over the heads of children, who were keener
on playing tig and hide-and-seek than listening
to the fowles' parliament; but when the bell
rang out for closing time, the darkness studied them
on their way home past the Dartry Dye Works.

The Magus

Simon rose into the sky, but was downed
By hostile spirits; was buried, but failed
To achieve his advertised resurrection.
They say his stolons rotted underground.

Or maybe he survived till he was eighty
And died in Antioch among his friends.
Conflicting tales; but all include Helena
And her reincarnations by a deity

In Troy and then as prostitute in Tyre,
Rescued by Simon Magus, who, obsessed
By her pale paranormal legs, dissolved
This world of angels and invited fire.

Now twin horse chestnuts shelter from the rain
Under their green cagoules, candles burned out:
With them in the dry, Simon, plus inhaler,
Alive to the significance of pain.

Not one of us, Simon; bit of a wimp
Say the forwards, outsider thinks the head;
He puzzles over magic texts and poems
(As though these could transmogrify a shrimp).

The boys throw sticks into the chestnut trees
To bring down their munitions for the autumn,
But Simon will not own or wield the champion,
His conkers will be victims of disease,

Sabotage, feebleness or Peter's prayer.
Time now to order another inhaler,
Get some colour into his tallow cheeks—
And then back to the games of solitaire

Till anagnorisis, foreseen in sleep,
Of the chilly-thighed adolescent girl,
Whose interest of course could not be roused—
Not for a sec, you dirty-minded creep.

In Shallow Water

Under the Salmon Weir Bridge in Galway
the grilse were driving themselves upriver.
Down on the quay men with extinct stubs
stuck to their unsmiling lower lips
were flogging eels to death on the granite—
running away to sea for their honeymoons,
they'd been waylaid by custom and cunning.
Then we flagged down the bus to Salthill
and got shelter from the wetting mist.

Those big eels seemed reluctant to die,
didn't they, dad? It took many flailings
before they would stay down for the count.
Their hearts had been set on the Sargasso
come what would. But something bigger came.
And the salmons' winning through was hardly
a pledge for them of tranquil retirement.
Do you think the eels will get well, dad,
or will they be eaten by those men?

I know, I know, time is what wounds heal in,
but not the eels' injuries, I fear.
Mashed potato and a sausage, that's
the lunch I got in the Salthill café
with its gritty floor and misted windows,
which I wiped with the sleeve of my jersey
to reveal a rainy wind-blown beach
where all the longshore fishermen's rods
held on to their standing invitations.

The Fever Hospital

The Boer War had broken out two weeks
Before Marjorie caught scarlet fever
And at the age of seven was rushed
In tears to an isolation hospital
Not far from the East India Docks.
Mother was playing at the Olympic
And father was embarking at Durban,
So the pretty, petted, youngest girl,
Temperature a hundred and four,
Lived out her delirium alone.

It left its mark on her, the world of stuff;
She suffered, felt herself abandoned, knew
The hay-filled pillow had to be burned
After her due discharge or decease.
The restless air smelled of carbolic, riverine
Fog crept in between the sashes, making
The ward like a cold and murky pond.
The nurses were not unkind, but discipline
Was looked for; God (this was before my time)
Was probably lurking just off-stage.

A scene for melodrama, perhaps,
But the damnation was real enough
For the hallucinating child, bed rolling
Like a trawler in a gale off Lowestoft,
Holding tight to the mattress's edge,
Fearful she might be swept overboard;
And the grey army blankets were so heavy—
Lead for wrapping around ancient corpses.
Unsleeping, her strawberry tongue felt
Sausage-like in her feverish mouth.

When she survived what was called the crisis,
Things steadied and interest lay elsewhere.
She was ordinary again, the air
Felt cool and calmative on her eyeballs,
The sick-room was just a place of tedium.
Later, among the bachelor's buttons
And the tightly pollarded lime trees
Of Clapham's macadamized side-streets,
There was the pleasure of those who knew her
And also their lack of curiosity.

Curtains

In the unlikely event of a breakdown
Do not stray far from your vehicle. Help
In the form of a man with big red hands
Will not be long in coming. He will bring
Heavy lifting equipment, metal cutters
And surgical instruments for emergencies.
He is a midwife as well as a rescuer;
If called upon he will deliver souls.

And a person carrying a raven's wing
May come your way with a reassuring smile,
Saying open wide, give me all you have,
You have no choice but to give without hope;
Oblivion may be just around the corner,
But you are barely into the home straight.
And there is no gainsaying him, it's true,
The wages of insolvency are pain.

Later in the hospital someone cries
Quick, nurse, quick, there is trouble in the making,
See, the old man in pyjamas and dressing gown
Has been taken bad again in the corridor;
He keeps on asking for love and freedom,
Which are things not even you can administer.
You must hush him up before he infects
The others with his refractory viruses.

Ouija

If the evidence is to be trusted
'Barnaby Wishford' presents himself
each time the aging friends get together
to raise a moistened forefinger cautiously
into the gale of the spirit world.

There is no billowing-out of curtains,
the flame of the night-light doesn't tremble,
the Cuban mahogany is steady.
The Ouija, though, has its hesitations,
trying to choose this letter or that.

Does uncertainty rise from the furniture
or is it a bias of the brains
where these open minds are bottled up?
Now the pointer shoots across the table,
moves once more to 'B', and then to 'A',

as it did last week, spells it all out
and pauses. U.N.H.A.P.P.Y, it says next;
but when questioned just repeats the name.
What are Cyril, Liz and Seán to do?
What entity has them in its sights?

Keep well clear of it, warn the advisers,
you will learn the secrets in your time,
when the other driver's claim for damages
has been thrown out of court and the crowd
has strolled away from the crematorium.

Untitled

Light streams from the east like a solar wind
And the old age pensioners sit in rows
Deep inside the hull of the parish church
As slaves sat at their oars in the Aegean.

But the galley is anchored fore and aft,
And the light flows over and past the chancel
Like river water splitting round a pier
And joins again, regardless of the hindrance.

Those inside are thinking about their ends
And the requiems they hope for, while the light
Goes on licking the slated roof above them
Like a domestic cat cleaning a saucer.

Like Minds

Of course you have no interest
In the condition of my fur-lined soul,
Nor I in that of yours.

Solids of revolution,
Artefacts without fingerprints or scratches
Might satisfy us both

But are in short supply.
The marks of aliens are all around us,
Attention-seeking curlicues,

Jewellery mixed with mucus,
An unwillingness to produce straight lines
When straight lines have been suggested

Or a determination
To draw lines straight against the best advice.
The hunger and treading down—

And the animus behind it!
But do you and I really care for feelingless
If perfect crystal spheres,

Whose lugubrious music
Is only wind keening around the dormers
As a low edges eastwards,

Impersonal as physics?
It's belonging to the cohort that matters,
Everyone else go hang.

And the delicious glue
That holds what were the boys and girls together
Is coded in Linear A,

Opaque to exegesis
As the diary of an iguanadon
To a mammalian reader.

Not that I look for empathy.
As I hinted, my soul is warm and snug,
Watching Petrushka's drama

In my private viewing room,
Though my tears form more slowly than they used to.
Maybe our tastes diverge,

But have I your attention?
Should I knock on the plasterboard and ask
Is anybody there?

This place is full of furniture
That I never have need of, and the skylight
Is useless to man or beast.

Around the Crater

The Cumaean Sibyl is washing her hair
But the smell of sulphur will not be shifted.
Vapour drifts over the Phlegraean Fields,
In Puteoli the ground cracks and rises,
Asphyxiated birds drop from the sky
Into the dull water of Lake Avernus.
Pilgrims arrive with offerings and care;

Throats still smarting from Solfatara's fumes
They drag their feet along the damp stone gallery,
Past the gatekeeper and the frowning guard,
Thinking up better words for their petitions;
But the day turns out to be inauspicious,
A sign declares the cave forbidden ground,
'The Sibyl is in trance among the tombs'.

Tomorrow the familiar crumpled leaves
Will float haphazardly out of the sanctum,
Bearing scraps of her automatic writing,
Whose hidden messages can be deciphered
For a consideration by a slyboots.
Fortune will soon be smiling on you, lady—
The riff-raff lose, the chosen one receives.

Shall we get out of here? A tremor rouses
The seekers from their futures to the present.
The Sibyl may be calm, but scalding steam
Blows noisily from the fumaroles, votive
Stones have tilted, the market is condemned;
Abandoned too the dwelling of the priest,
He whose tenets we'd thought as safe as houses.

Some warblers in an ilex, lost for words,
Fill in with the equivalent of rhubarb
To pass the time in the Astroni crater,
Where sorcerers' noses can still detect
A sulphurous history in the wind;
They shun the ground, unlike the snakes and certain
Not very bright (but brightly coloured) birds.

Summer Night

A false dawn radiates from vaguely east
And the atmosphere is holding its breath.
Every leaf is still, spellbound in its place,
As in Victorian photographs of shrubberies,
Foregrounds taken up by full-skirted ladies
Marked by their knowledge of infant mortality,
The barely formed skeletons at the feast.

Each night the population goes to sleep
As though felled by asphyxiating gases
Or hot ashes blown out of a volcano.
They look like Everyman caught in Pompeii.
In dull suburban bedrooms I have seen
Simulacra of suicides or victims
Fallen from the parapet of a keep,

Or so they looked—the arms and legs awry,
Paralysed in postures of tribulation,
Heads thrown back in extremis, torsos twisted.
And a basilisk must haunt the children's room;
Its glare is what the small boy cowered away from,
Like one who flung himself down on a rugby ball
To halt a pack of behemoths or die.

Elsewhere I've seen a Botticelli face,
Limbs unstrung like a puppet's, perhaps accepting
The attentions of a visiting incubus.
And all laid out, inert and horizontal,
A town full of silently busy brains,
Self-exiled from the world of geese and goosegrass,
Ruled by imaginary time and space.

But as we move from shadow into light
The automatons will resume their cycles,
The ballet-dancer pirouette perpetually,
And the fiddler, chin-rest tucked under smile,
Will play his single tune, look for applause,
Play it again and look around again
With his insatiable appetite.

Alessandro Moreschi, Castrato

When he was ten they snipped his little balls off,
This being in everyone's interest, including God's.
Now, said Padre Matteo, his angelic voice
Will save us all. Alesso was not consulted.

Today I heard it, the boyish treble that survived
The iron maiden of the twentieth century,
Still sparkling like acqua minerale con gas.
'Ave Maria!', he thinly trilled, 'Ave Maria!'.

Breakfast Time

The morning curtain rises and the scene's the same
     Just as it was at yesterday's nightfall.
The air sits with its hands in its lap, like water
     In a blue deserted swimming-pool,
The lime tree's branches are hushing the orchestra,
     The bird-box has yet to find a tenant
And a treecreeper spirals swiftly up the trunk

And up another trunk, and again, again,
     As it did yesterday and will do
Tomorrow and next year, whenever that may be.
     And I look out as I looked out yesterday
(Or was it the day before?) and my coffee cools
     And the sun squints round the Cryptomeria
Into whose foliage vert the night has sunk.

A postman now enters by the gate, stage left,
     Singing the intro in a light tenor,
But where are the smiling girls with their round thighs,
     The coarse-grained comedians, the villain
And the principal boy with her beautiful bosom?
     Why is the music so rallentando
And each performance slower than the last?

Someone-or-other's clock needs winding up.
     Anyway the postman is running late
And his billets-doux cool in the early sun.
     A letter shot through the door contains
Some message from the tribe, welcome or not,
     And its solicitings or affection
Will take me into the future or the past.

II

On Wexford Bridge

i.m. J. H. Colclough

I

When I was a small boy my relatives
Had a skeleton in their mental cupboard
That was not referred to except
Through slips of the tongue at mealtimes,
And these incurred frowns of reproof.

When brain death overcame these elders
The skeleton had to move house
And, finding himself in the sunlight,
Surprised us all when he was greeted
Right and left as a martyred patriot.

Death by hanging could now be mentioned,
Even boasted of, as though virtue
Could be gained by association -
We had genes in common with 'A Leader
Of Seventeen Ninety-Eight'.

II

I, John Henry Colclough, am the subject
Of those attention-seeking stanzas.
But it's for me, now in my timelessness,
To reflect on those dreadful months
When we were chewed up and disgorged.

We were 'three respectable gentlemen
Of the County of Wexford', Edward
Fitzgerald, Beauchamp Bagenal Harvey

And myself (a qualified physician),
All landowners in a modest way

And 'men of liberal principles',
Troubled by injustices inflicted
On our neighbours—townsfolk, small farmers,
Their hired hands, most of them Catholic,
But God's creatures for all that—

And terrified of the bands of Orangemen,
The bigots with their so-called loyalty
To the unloved couple from Holland.
In their eyes Papists' bodies looked well
On gallows and roadside gibbets;

Tolerance was midwife to treason.
Many events were veiled by storms
And whirlwinds were whisked up by passion,
Veering unpredictably here
And there with their acts of undoing.

III

Seventeen ninety-eight, and the Quakers
Were founding their school in Waterford,
But most minds were on the Orange devils,
Ravaging the townlands for provender
And the subjugation of idolaters.

The military were in tumult,
Coming and going and saving their skins
At the cost of firearms and howitzers
Lost to the insurrectionists.
General Fawcett scurried back

To the grey fortress in Duncannon,
Having lost his men and matériel
At the rebel-held Three Rocks,
Which caused Colonel Maxwell to feel shame
But pull his own men back to Wexford.

The Donegal militia hanged
Four prisoners in Clonegall,
Though the gentlemen of the town
Spoke up for them as loyal citizens.
That took Lieutenant Young, the Duty

Officer, two hours to accomplish.
Under a soft blue sky, with cloudlets
Drifting peacefully across from Clare,
Pigs were observed in Gorey's streets
To eat the bodies of insurgents

Recently shot, some still expiring.
And while a soft wind brushed his cheek
A soldier fired into a bush,
Dragged out a screaming boy of eight,
Six other children and their mother.

Hearing of this my wife cried aloud
And my children, knowing they were weak
And scared by such uncensored feelings,
Slipped away to the back of the paddock
To a hiding-place in the ha-ha.

Rumours flickered like summer lightning,
Wild crowds streamed into market places,
Howling and drunk on looted spirits;
There was no rule and no safe keeping,
The cabins' thatch went up in flames.

Heroics, glamour and romance
Were, as always, the absentee darlings;
In truth, on all sides, chaos and savagery
(Called manliness by misanthropes),
Wound up in unbridled cruelty.

IV

But the red cows had to be milked
And the mushrooms went on growing
In the long green grass, where the horses
(Or those that had not been stolen),
Still stood around flicking their tails.

The dung-flies went about their business
In the shade of the hawthorn hedges,
Unaware of of the rage and fear
That poisoned the last week of May
And evacuated many bowels.

V

From information received and
On the 'suspicion of treasonable
Designs', a Captain Boyd arrested
Harvey, Fitzgerald and myself;
And threw us into Wexford prison.

What information? From what source?
This was not revealed, but ill-will
And slander is the likely answer.
We had not hidden our contempt
For all harsh upstart Orangemen.

But under pressure at the drumhead
Edward Fitzgerald and myself,
Though forbidden to offer terms,
Agreed to ride to Enniscorthy
To parley with the mutinous crowd

And urge them back to their homes.
It was an anxious day of ridng
Through mist and challenges and threats,
But when we fetched up at Vinegar Hill
The crowd, though restless and distracted

And at cross purposes among themselves,
Agreed to hear me out in silence;
When I had said my say the rebels
Disputed at the tops of their voices,
Mixing arguments and abuse

Like oil and kindling, with the hotheads
Throwing the last word, the flaming match.
Somehow through all that argy-bargy
They resolved to march at once on Wexford—
But to detain my friend Fitzgerald.

Back in Wexford's bull ring, on horseback,
I, playing Stentor, owned our failure
To sway the the will of the insurgents—
Soon to arrive with pikes and forks.
Then in fulfilment of my promise

I took Bagenal Harvey's place in gaol.
There followed frenzy and confusion,
The town stormed and plundered, fired,
All prisoners released, green boughs
Hung up as emblems of insurgency,

Fleeing troops massacring the peasants—
Suffering that cannot be thought of
(And in those days no one spoke of rape).
But when retaken by the military,
The principal citizens were gaoled

And formally arraigned for treason.
Harvey, myself and our true wives
Fled by boat to the Saltee Islands,
Hoping to weather out the storms
Of that fearful time in a cave.

But Protestant cleanliness betrayed us
When laundry laid out on the rocks
By our particular spouses
Was spotted from a passing cutter
And a message passed post-haste to Wexford.

So we were discovered and brought back,
Watched by a crowd on Kilmore Quay,
Whence we two men were led to gaol
And the condemned cells, to await
Court martial and its foregone ending.

Traitors, found guilty of commitment
To the abolition of bigotry
Through the arm of the United Irishmen,
We and the others were condemned.
Harvey was hanged on Wexford Bridge,

His body stripped and treated
'With the usual brutal indecencies'
(Words that mean 'hanged, drawn and quartered')
And his head transfixed on a pike.
Then I, after incontinent panic

And that most terrible paroxysm,
Looked down and saw myself
Hanging from a scaffold on the bridge.
(Smile if you will, but I wish to say
That as a gentleman I'd been allowed

To wear my coat during the ritual.)
At the pleading of my dearest wife
I saw my corpse delivered up to her,
Laid out and taken away by cart
To Ballyteigue for decent burial.

Others that day—Grogan, Kelly, Keogh—
Died under even greater savagery.
Fitzgerald, though, became a leader
At Vinegar Hill, fought and surrendered
And lived to end his days in Hamburg.

VI

As always is the way
The players knew their parts
But could not see the play;
And neither brains nor hearts
Yesterday or today
Can explicate the kinds
Of fissures that ran through
The crystals of the minds
And eyes of those that slew.
Hate ulcerates and blinds.

1922, early evening:
Miss Colclough sits in the drawing-room
Of her house, built into the ruins
Of Tintern Abbey, Wexford. What-nots
In mother-of-pearl, and Union flags;

Miss Colclough's skirts trail on the floor,
A modesty vest conceals her poverty.
Knock on the door, to which she goes,
Opens and sees the skyline lit
By flames from burning country houses.

An open car parked on the gravel,
Men in the trench coats of convention,
The IRA of course. 'Miss Colclough,
We know of that fine man, your cousin,
John Henry Colclough—have no fear,

Your home will be spared, you may sleep
And dream of an Ireland being born.'
And so it was. My father snapped her
In 1933, the Union flag
Still aloft in the drawing-room—

A mild old lady in a tea gown,
Keeping up her strange appearances,
Having made a truce with a past
That it was painful to think about
But painful to think of forgetting.

Notes

Cheap Music, p. 25
[Nuwara Eliya: pron. <u>Nu</u>war <u>Ai</u>lya, almost without a break]

Bougainvillea, p. 28
de Bougainville (1729-1811), avocat, adjutant, secrétaire d'ambassade, membre agrégé de la Société Royale de Londres, capitaine reformé, colonel, chevalier de Saint-Louis, capitaine de frégate et de vaisseau, navigateur au long cours, chef d'escadre, maréchal de camp, vice-amiral, membre de l'Institut, compte de l'Empire, chevalier de la Légion d'honeur.

Printed in the United Kingdom
by Lightning Source UK Ltd.
108822UKS00001BB/127-288